NANCY

BIRTHDAY

WIS HES

WITH LOVE,

JILL

·2001·

CELEBRATIONS

A year of Parties, Extravaganzas, & Gatherings with Friends & Family

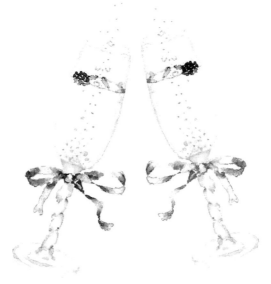

SUSAN BRANCH

CEDCO PUBLISHING
SAN RAFAEL, CALIFORNIA

ISBN 0-7683-2197-2

Published in 2000 by Cedco Publishing Company
100 Pelican Way, San Rafael, California 94901
For a free catalog of other Cedco® products,
please write to the address above,
or visit their website : www.cedco.com

PRINTED IN SINGAPORE

1 3 5 7 9 10 8 6 4 2

"THEREFORE ALL
SEASONS
SHALL BE SWEET
TO THEE..."
♥ Samuel Taylor Coleridge

Spring is magic ~
sweet to the senses
& easy to celebrate.

Spring is heard as much as seen.

occasion   date

occasion _____ date _____

In Like a Lion
Out Like a Lamb

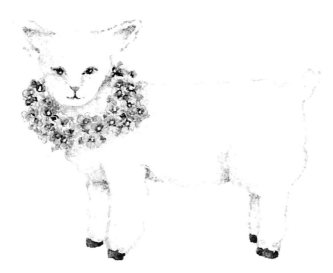

occasion

May this sweetest
old-time greeting,
Heavily laden with
good cheer,

Bring content and
peace and plenty,
To last throughout
the year. ♥

occasion

date

occasion _____ date _____
_____
_____
_____
_____
_____
_____
_____
_____
_____
_____

occasion

date

"There are strange evenings
when the flowers have a soul."

occasion _____ date _____

occasion _____ date _____

It's
Spring
again
and
Birds on
the

Wing Again
Start to Sing
'AGAIN'

Love's Sweet
Melody...

occasion _____ date _____

"I thought that spring must last for ever more —
For I was young, and loved, and it was May." ♥
Vera Brittain

occasion _____   date

"Life itself is the proper binge."
♥ Julia Child

occasion _____ date

"DON'T HURRY, DON'T WORRY. YOU'RE ONLY HERE FOR A SHORT VISIT. SO BE SURE TO STOP AND SMELL THE FLOWERS."
Walter C. Hagen

"We had mighty good weather as a general thing, & nothing ever happened to us at all." *Mark Twain*

occasion _____ date _____

_____

_____

_____

_____

_____

_____

_____

_____

_____

_____

_____

"*Never eat more than you can lift.*"

♥ MISS PIGGY

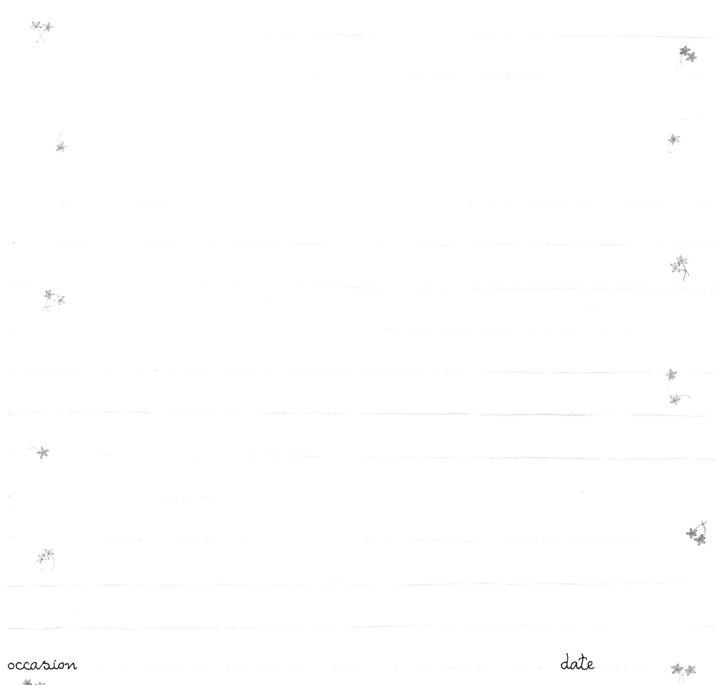

occasion   date

"To invite a person into your house is to take charge of his happiness for as long as he is under your roof." A. Brillat-Savarin ~ ♥

'The fair maid who, the first of May
Goes to the fields at break of day
And washes in dew from the hawthorn tree,
Will ever after handsome be.'

occasion _____

date _____

occasion _____ date

occasion _____   date

♥ It's spring, so sing ♪!

occasion _____ date _____

glue photo
here

"In all things of nature there is
something of the marvelous." ♥
Aristotle

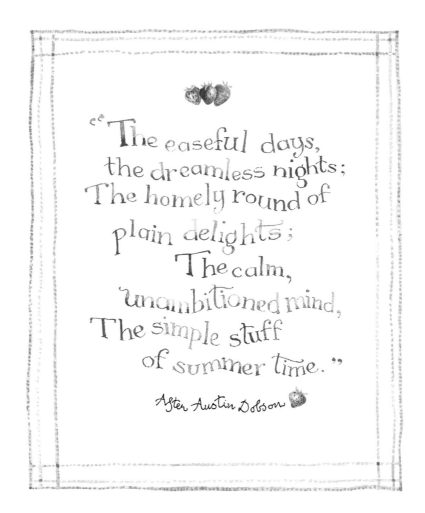

"The easeful days,
the dreamless nights;
The homely round of
plain delights;
The calm,
unambitioned mind,
The simple stuff
of summer time."

After Austin Dobson

SUMMER
CELEBRATIONS

"Summer afternoon — summer afternoon; to me those have always been the two most beautiful words in the English language." ♥ Henry James

occasion   date

occasion   date

"Prone to revenge, the bees,
a wrathful race..."

Samuel Bagster

...but, oh! Honey!

occasion _____   date _____

occasion _____   date

I LOVE SUMMERZZZ

occasion   date

"I am not a gourmet chick." ♥ Pearl Bailey

occasion   date

occasion _____   date _____

occasion _____   date _____

"Long live the sun
which gives us such color."
♥ Paul Cézanne

occasion   date

"What is patriotism but the love of the good things we ate in our childhood?"
♥ Lin Yutang

JULY 4TH PICNIC

occasion   date

"THE SUNSHINE SEEMED TO BLESS,
THE AIR WAS A CARESS." 💙   John Greenleaf Whittier

HOUSEWORK, WHEN DONE CORRECTLY,
CAN KILL YOU. ♡

WHAT YOU EAT
STANDING UP
DOESN'T COUNT. ♥

occasion   date

occasion   date

CAMPING

occasion   date

A
picnic
is
a state
of mind
&
can be
made
anywhere.

occasion　　　　　　　　　　　　　　　date

occasion _____   date

"What dreadful hot weather we have!
It keeps me in a continual state of
inelegance." ❤ Jane Austen

occasion

date

THE STRAWBERRY
Nature's Valentine

occasion _____ date _____

"I'm trying to arrange my life so that I don't even have to be present." ♥ Anonymous

"THEY AREN'T LONG, THE DAYS OF WINE AND ROSES!" ♥ E. DOWSON

occasion

date

"No Spring, nor Summer Beauty
hath such grace,
As I have seen
in one Autumnall face."
♥ John Donne

FALL

FESTIVITIES

"WHEN THE DAYS BEGIN TO
SHORTEN, SOON AFTER SOLSTICE
ON JUNE 21, A TREE RECONSIDERS
ITS LEAVES."

A NATURAL HISTORY OF THE SENSES

occasion _____ date _____

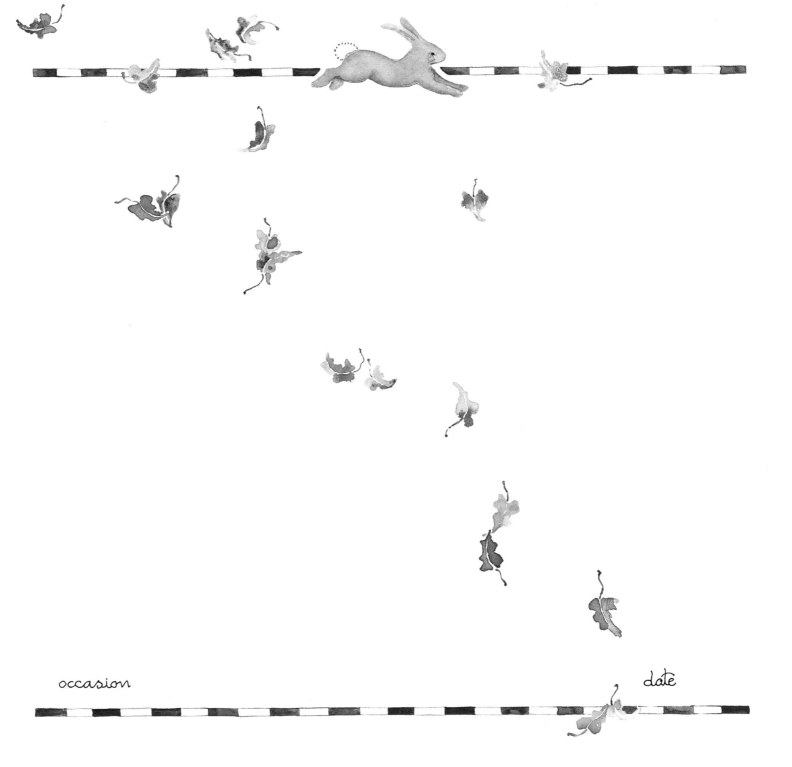

occasion

date

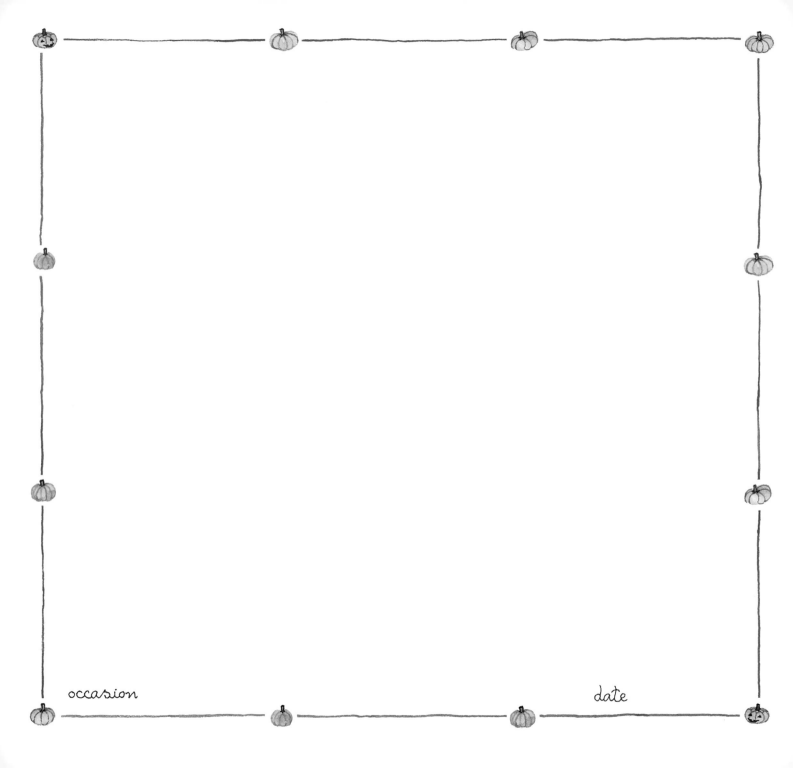

occasion   date

"I would rather sit on a pumpkin and have it all to myself than be crowded on a velvet cushion." ~ H. Thoreau

occasion _____ date _____

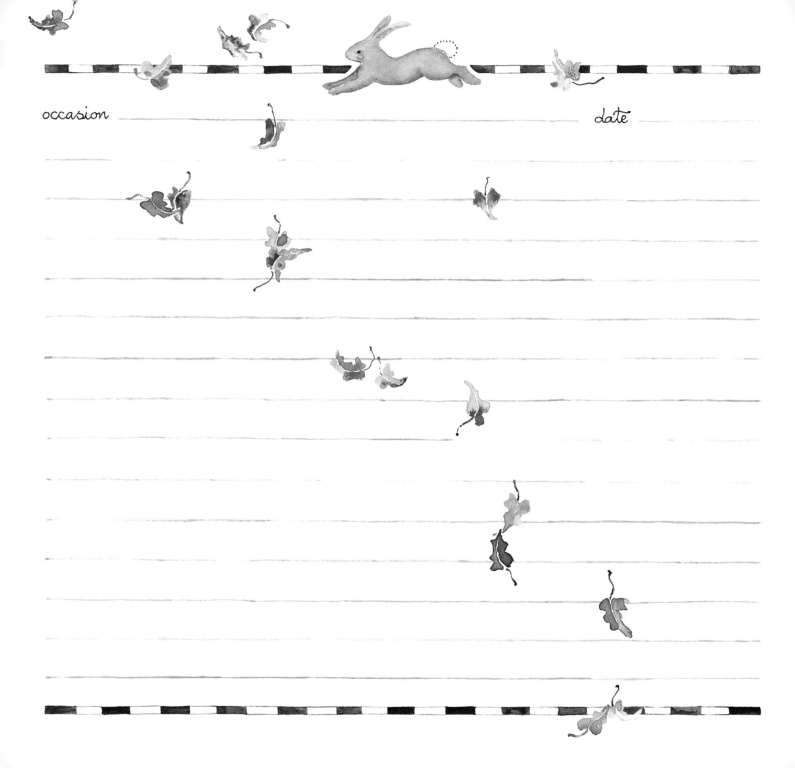

occasion _____ date

"Thank God for tea! What would the world do without tea? — how did it exist? I am glad I was not born before tea." ♥ Sydney Smith

occasion _____ date _____

SOOTHES NERVES. ♥ 'BURNED OUT' BLOOD? NO PROBLEM — MIX HONEY WITH INFUSED SASSAFRAS BARK & VOILÀ!

HONEY FOR TEA ♥ HONEY TO TASTE. ♥

YOU'RE CURED. ♥ BEE KISSES ♥ WARM 2 C. HONEY & MIX IT WITH 7 SPRIGS OF THYME. SPREAD ON BISCUITS.

FLOWER NECTAR FOR WAFFLES & CORN BREAD, MIX SOFTENED BUTTER WITH

occasion   date

FLU? JUICE OF 1 LEMON, SHOT OF WHISKEY, SPOON OF HONEY INTO HOT WATER. GOODNIGHT.

occasion   date

" We live in deeds, not years; in thoughts, not breaths; in feelings, not in figures on a dial.
We should count time by heart-throbs. He most lives who thinks most ~
feels the noblest ~ acts the best."
                                                                P.J. Bailey ♥

occasion   date

AND THE GOBLINS'LL GIT YOU IF YOU DON'T WATCH OUT!

occasion

date

occasion   date

"I believe in festival days with all my
heart. I think we should sometimes
call our friends together, and
give them bright thoughts for
the intellect, friendliness for
the heart, and good things for
the palate." ❤ A.M. Diaz

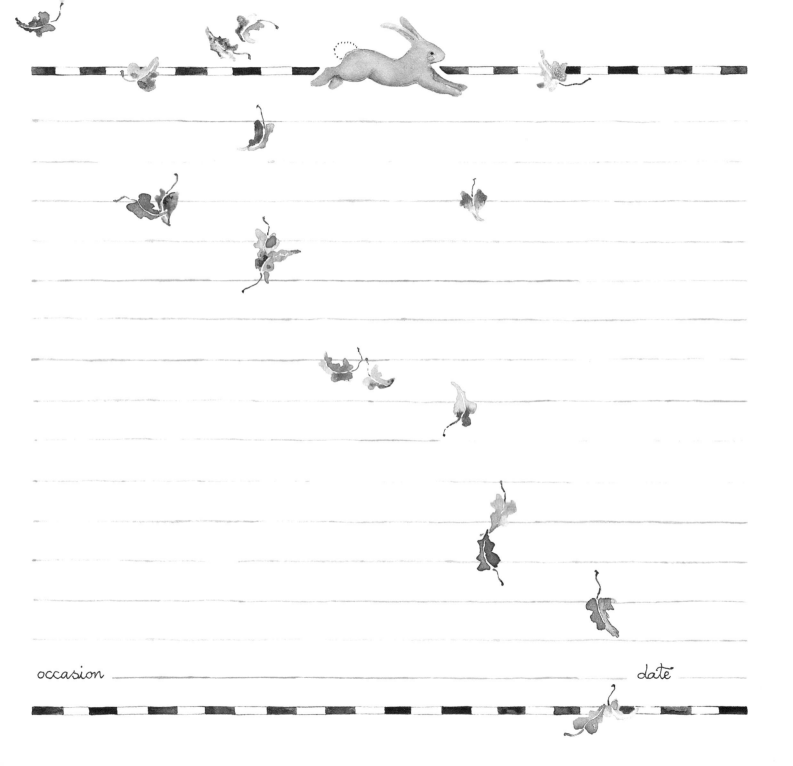

occasion _____ date _____

"Once in a young lifetime one should be allowed to
   have as much sweetness as one can possibly want
& hold."
                    ♡ Judith Olney

COME & GET IT!

occasion   date

" I never see any home cooking.
All I get is fancy stuff."
Duke of Edinburgh

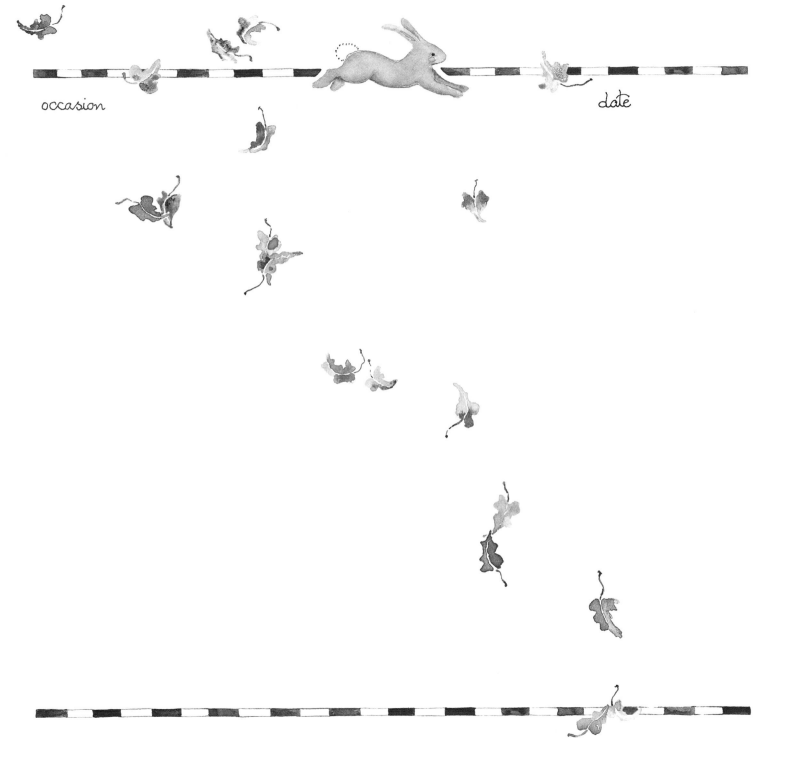

occasion

date

"He that is of a merry heart hath a continual feast."

♥ Proverbs 15:15

occasion   date

"So once in every year we throng
Upon a day apart,
To praise the Lord with feast and song
In thankfulness of heart." ♥
Arthur Guiterman

occasion _____ date _____

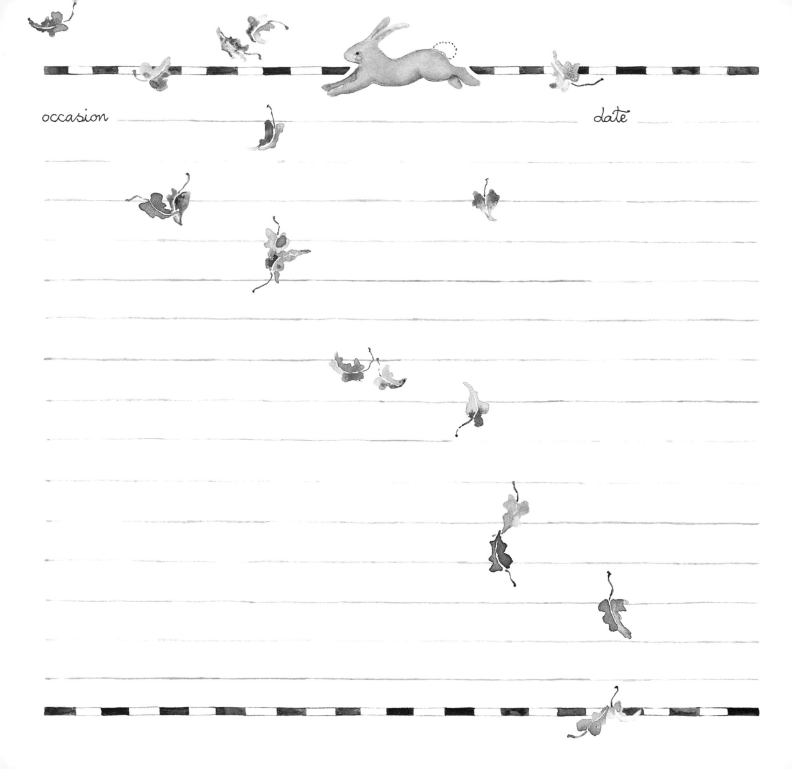

occasion _____ date

" There's absolutely no reason for being
rushed along with the rush. Everybody
should be free to go very slow. "

Robt. Frost

occasion _____ date _____

occasion _____   date _____

"Happiness grows at our own firesides, and
is not to be picked in strangers' gardens."
♥ Douglas Jerrold ♥

O winter,
King of
Intimate
Delights...

"The height of luxury was reached in the
winter afternoons... lying in a tin bath
in front of a coal fire, drinking tea,
and eating well-buttered crumpets...."
♥ J. C. Masterman

occasion _____   date _____

occasion _____ date _____

"A dinner invitation, once accepted, is a sacred obligation. If you die before the dinner takes place, your executor must attend."

♡ Ward McAllister

IT'S NOT WHAT'S ON THE PLATES THAT MATTERS. IT'S WHAT'S ON THE CHAIRS.

occasion _____   date _____

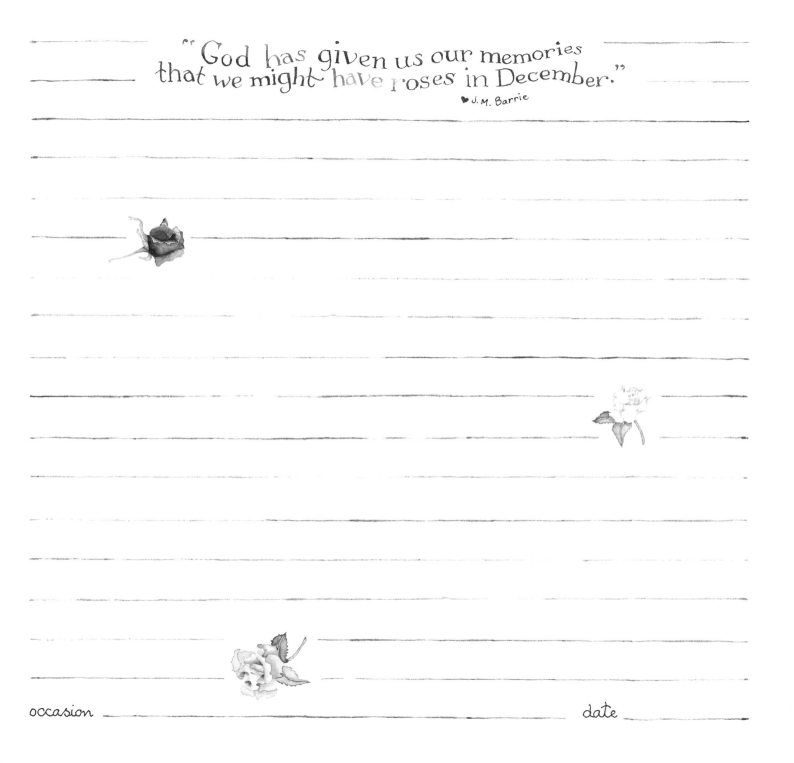

"God has given us our memories
that we might have roses in December."
♥ J. M. Barrie

occasion _____ date _____

occasion _____   date _____

WINTER MEMORIES

occasion _____ date _____

"Come in the evening,
come in the morning,
Come when expected,
come without warning;
Thousands of welcomes
you'll find here before you,
And the oftener you come,
the more we'll adore you."
♥ Irish Rhyme

occasion   date

occasion _____ date _____

"Close by the jolly fire I sit
To warm my frozen bones a bit."
Robt. Louis Stevenson ♥

There's NO BUSINESS LIKE
SNOW BUSINESS, LIKE
NO BUSINESS I KNOW_"

Sandra Boynton

THE MAGIC

OF SNOW

"Backward, turn backward, O Time in your flight;
Make me a child again just for tonight."
                                    Elizabeth Akers Allen

occasion _____   date _____

occasion _____   date _____

_____

_____

_____

_____

_____

_____

_____

_____

_____

_____

_____

_____

_____

occasion _____ date _____

"For somehow, not only at Christmas, but all the long year through, the joy that you give to others is the joy that comes back to you."
♥ John Greenleaf Whittier

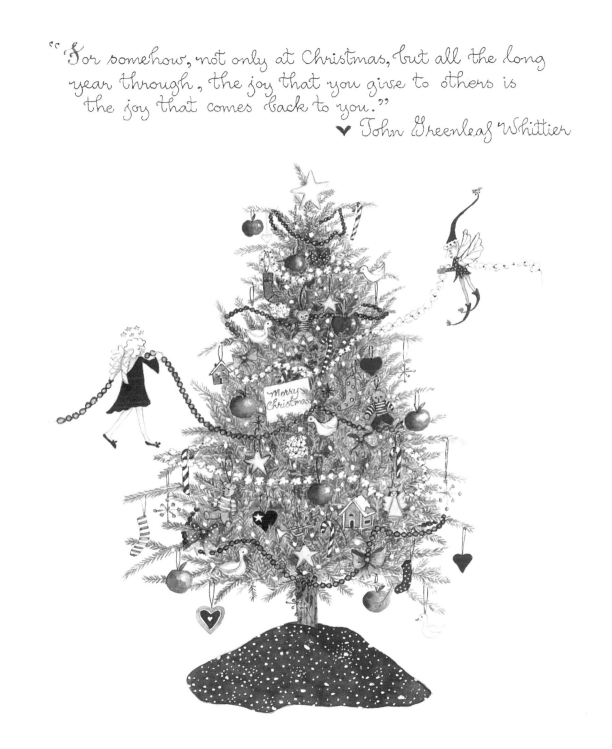

occasion _____ date

A LITTLE NONSENSE NOW & THEN
IS RELISHED BY THE WISEST MEN.

occasion _____ date _____

HAPPY NEW YEAR

occasion _____   date _____

occasion _____   date _____

"O, COME QUICKLY, I AM DRINKING STARS!"

So sayeth Dom Perignon upon his discovery of Champagne

occasion _____ date _____

"The cold wind burns my face,
and blows
It's frosty pepper up my nose."
Robt. Louis Stevenson

MMMMMM

♡ Life is short, eat dessert first ♡

occasion _____   date _____

_____

_____

_____

_____

_____

_____

_____

_____

_____

The love in your heart wasn't put there to stay,
love isn't love till it's given away.

occasion   date

occasion _____   date _____

"On with the dance!
Let joy be unconfined."
♥ Lord Byron

occasion _____   date _____

occasion   date

" . . . our life is what our
thoughts make it."
♥ Marcus Aurelius